T0329209

OEDIPUS AT COLONUS

CAMBRIDGE
UNIVERSITY PRESS

University Printing House, Cambridge CB2 8BS, United Kingdom

Published in the United States of America by Cambridge University Press, New York

Cambridge University Press is part of the University of Cambridge.

It furthers the University's mission by disseminating knowledge in the pursuit of
education, learning and research at the highest international levels of excellence.

www.cambridge.org
Information on this title: www.cambridge.org/9781107634282

© Cambridge University Press 1946

First published 1946
Re-issued 2014

A catalogue record for this publication is available from the British Library

ISBN 978-1-107-63428-2 Paperback

TRANSLATIONS BY R. C. TREVELYAN

EURIPIDES: MEDEA
AESCHYLUS: PROMETHEUS BOUND
VIRGIL: THE ECLOGUES & THE GEORGICS
LUCRETIUS: DE RERUM NATURA
Translations from HORACE, JUVENAL, MONTAIGNE
Translations from LEOPARDI

SOPHOCLES
OEDIPUS AT COLONUS

TRANSLATED BY

R. C. TREVELYAN

CAMBRIDGE
AT THE UNIVERSITY PRESS
1946

To

GORDON AND TEETEE LUCE

INTRODUCTION

Sophocles died at the age of 90 in the year 406 B.C. The *Oedipus at Colonus* is generally considered to have been written in his old age, and according to one ancient authority it was first produced by the poet's grandson four years after his death.

I cannot hope to give any account of this difficult and much discussed play that has not already been better given by others; so I will quote a few sentences written by Dr J. T. Sheppard, with which I find myself in complete sympathy.

'The *Oedipus at Colonus* is a patriotic and religious mystery. The hero, after a life of shame and persecution, is received by Athens, welcomed in spite of his past, defended against the enemies of his own household, and vindicated in the end by the gods. Throughout the play there grows on the hero and the audience a sense that his tragic life has not been altogether without purpose. There is no shallow explanation, and not even the suggestion that the fires of passion have been purged by suffering. Oedipus curses his sons: Antigone, not Oedipus, was born for love. Oedipus is no saint, no Christian hero, but a man who feels himself abnormal, charged by his tragedy with a mysterious potency for good and evil to friends and foes. Athens receives him when the rest of the world rejects him. She defends him in his weakness. She shall find safety from his strength. The drama culminates in his majestic passage from the life of men.'*

It may also be of interest to transcribe the following note which was pencilled by Macaulay in the Sophocles which he took with him to India in 1834.

'I cannot quite agree with Schlegel in putting this play at the head of Sophocles's plays. There is great sweetness both of sentiment and style, great and noble national enthusiasm, and a fine religious solemnity thrown over the whole. Theseus is the model of ancient heroes; Antigone and Ismene are most touch-

* *Aeschylus and Sophocles, their work and influence*, by J. T. Sheppard, Litt.D. George G. Harrap & Co. Ltd.

ingly represented. But from a boy I always found the play a little languid, particularly the scenes with Creon and Polyneices.'

I do not myself find the Creon and Polyneices episodes to be 'languid'. Lengthy, no doubt, they are; and neither of them lead up to a momentous dramatic crisis, as such scenes generally do in the other works of Sophocles. But the unity of this play is not that of a close-knit plot ruthlessly developing step by step towards disastrous catastrophe. Here the sequence of incidents, exciting and picturesque, passionate and pathetic, are all parts of the leisurely movement towards the mysterious passing of Oedipus, which is one of the greatest things in dramatic poetry.

In no other play has Sophocles shown himself a greater master of poetic expression and atmosphere. The characters, Oedipus and Polyneices, Theseus and Creon, are convincingly portrayed and contrasted; and there is a beautiful delicacy in the relations of Antigone with her father, brother, and sister, of a kind that may hardly be found elsewhere in Greek drama.

In Greek poetry the metrical design is determined by the length and shortness of the syllables, not by the stress, as in English verse. If we wish to reproduce a Greek rhythmical phrase in English, we must, as it were, translate quantity into stress. At the same time, where possible, long and short English syllables must correspond to long and short Greek syllables. When translating the lyrics and anapaests of Greek plays, I have hitherto attempted to imitate as closely as possible the metrical pattern and phrasing of the original; and such had been my intention when I began to translate the *Oedipus at Colonus*. But in several of the choruses I found the Greek rhythms so difficult to reproduce in English verse that it seemed better here to give up the attempt, rather than do violence to the phrasing and diction for the sake of a theory. The choruses which I have rendered into freer verse-forms are the last two stanzas of the first stasimon, lines 694–719; the second stasimon, lines 1044–1095; and the fourth stasimon, lines 1556–1578.

I have translated from the text published by Professor Jebb in 1900, and have numbered the lines in accordance with that edition.

6

DRAMATIS PERSONAE

OEDIPUS
ANTIGONE, *his daughter*
A STRANGER
ISMENE, *daughter of Oedipus*
THESEUS, *King of Athens*
CREON, *King of Thebes*
POLYNEICES, *son of Oedipus*
A MESSENGER
CHORUS *of Elders of Colonus*

OEDIPUS AT COLONUS

OEDIPUS

Child of the blind old man, Antigone,
To what land have we come? Whose city is this?
Who is it that today shall entertain
The wanderer Oedipus with niggard gifts?
Little do I beg for; and less than that little
Do I obtain; but that suffices me:
For sufferings and the schooling of long years,
And lastly pride of birth have taught me patience.
Now, child, if any resting-place you see,
Whether on profane ground or in some God's grove,   10
Lead me and seat me there, that we may enquire
Where we are; for we needs must learn as strangers
From denizens, and act as they may bid.

ANTIGONE

Father, long-suffering Oedipus, the towers
That guard the city appear far distant still.
And holy, it seems, this place must be, thick-set
With laurel, olive, vine: and nightingales
Thronging within it make sweet melody.
Here rest your limbs upon this unhewn stone.
For one so old a long way have you journeyed.   20

OEDIPUS

Then seat me here, and watch over my blindness.

ANTIGONE

That task after so long I need not learn.

OEDIPUS

Can you now tell me whither we are come?

ANTIGONE

Athens yonder I know, but not this place.

OEDIPUS

So much we learnt from every passer-by.

ANTIGONE
Then shall I go and learn how the place is called?

OEDIPUS
Do so, my child, if it be inhabited.

ANTIGONE
It must be.—But I think there is no need...
For yonder not far off I see a man.

OEDIPUS
Someone coming towards us from the village?   30

ANTIGONE
Already he stands beside us. You must speak
Whatever the moment prompts; for the man is here.

Enter STRANGER, *a man of Colonus*

OEDIPUS
Sir, warned by her who sees both for herself
And me, that you have come thus opportunely
To make enquiry and to resolve our doubts...

STRANGER
Before you question further, quit this seat.
You have entered ground 'tis sacrilege to tread.

OEDIPUS
What ground is this? held sacred to what deity?

STRANGER
None may enter nor dwell there; for those dread
Goddesses hold it, daughters of Earth and Darkness.   40

OEDIPUS
Say by what awful name should I invoke them.

STRANGER
The all-seeing Eumenides the folk here
Would call them: other names elsewhere seem best.

OEDIPUS
Now graciously may they receive their suppliant;
For my seat in this land never will I quit.

STRANGER
What means this?

10

OEDIPUS

'Tis the watchword of my fate.

STRANGER

Well, hence I dare not drive you, till I report
My purpose, and receive the city's sanction.

OEDIPUS

Now by the Gods, kind Sir, refuse me not
That knowledge I, sad wanderer, crave of thee.   50

STRANGER

What would you know? Speak; I will not refuse you.

OEDIPUS

What then is the place called that we have entered?

STRANGER

Listen, and you shall learn all that I know.
Sacred is this whole place. Revered Poseidon
Holds it, and the fire-breathing God, the Titan
Prometheus. But the spot whereon you tread
Is called the Brazen Threshold of this land,
The stay of Athens; and the neighbouring fields
Make it their boast that their primordial lord
Was yonder knight Colonos, and all the folk   60
Yet bear his name in common for their own.
Such, stranger, are these haunts, less famed in story
Than honoured by the love of those who dwell there.

OEDIPUS

Then there are folk inhabiting this place?

STRANGER

Aye, called by yonder divine hero's name.

OEDIPUS

Have they a king? or does the whole people rule?

STRANGER

This region is governed by the city's king.

OEDIPUS

Who is sovereign here in counsel and in might?

11

STRANGER
Theseus, son to Aegeus, who once reigned.

OEDIPUS
Could a messenger be sent by you to find him?   70

STRANGER
For what purpose? To urge him to come hither?

OEDIPUS
That by small service he may win great gain.

STRANGER
What benefit can come from one who sees not?

OEDIPUS
In all that I shall speak there will be vision.

STRANGER
Mark me now, friend, lest you should come to harm—
For despite evil fortune you seem noble—
Stay here, where I first found you, till I go
And make report to the demesmen of this village,
Not in the city. They it is must decide
Whether you should remain here or depart.   *Exit.*   80

OEDIPUS
Are we alone, my child? Has the man gone?

ANTIGONE
He is gone; so with a tranquil mind, father,
You may speak what you will. I only am near you.

OEDIPUS
Holy Powers of dread aspect, since you first
Have given me a seat to rest on in this land,
To Phoebus and to me prove not ungracious.
When he announced my doom of countless woes,
This resting place after long years he promised.
Reaching my goal in a land where the Awful Goddesses
Would grant me shelter and hospitality,   90
There I should close my miserable life,
With benefits for those who welcomed me,
But ruin for them who drove me forth an outcast.

12

And of these things, signs, so he warned, would come,
Earthquake, or thunder and lightning from the sky.
Now I perceive that it can be naught else
Than some truthful omen from you, which thus
Has led me to this grove. How else could I
Have met with you first in my wanderings—
I, the austere, with you that love not wine—   100
Or have set me down upon this holy seat
Shaped by no tool of man? Then, Goddesses,
According to Apollo's word, grant me
Some way to close my course and end my life,
If I seem not beneath such grace, enslaved
To the worst miseries mortals can endure.
Hear, kindly daughters of primeval Darkness!
Hear, thou who art called the dwelling of great Pallas,
Athens, among all cities first in honour!
Pity this wretched ghost of Oedipus;
For he, the man who once was, is no more.   110

ANTIGONE
Silence! Some aged men I see coming
To seek you out here in your resting-place.

OEDIPUS
I will be silent. But lead me from the road
And hide me in the wood, till I have heard
What the men may be saying. For us strangers
It were but prudent first to learn their mood.

They retire into the wood. Enter CHORUS.

CHORUS
Search—who was he? Where does he lurk?   *Strophe 1*
Where has he stolen away, this wretch, of all men
The most shameless and insolent?   120
On all sides scan the grove;
With keen eyes peer around.
A wanderer
That old man—from afar he comes—
A stranger; for he ne'er had else
Dared approach the untrodden wood

13

Where the terrible maidens dwell,
Whose very name we dread to speak:
With averted eyes we pass by,   130
With lips moving without a sound,
No word spoken, in silent awe
Of worship. Now we are told that one
Is come who reveres them in no wise.
But of him naught yet can I see, though I search
Far and wide through the grove.
I know not where he is hiding.

OEDIPUS, *coming forward with* ANTIGONE
I am he that you seek. By sound do I see,
As they say of the blind.

CHORUS
O! O!   140
Dread sight to behold, voice fearful to hear!

OEDIPUS
Nay, I beseech you, deem me not lawless.

CHORUS
Zeus warder of evil! who is this old man?

OEDIPUS
One not so fortunate as to deserve
Your envy, O guardians of this land.
'Tis plain: else ne'er by another's eyes
Thus were I walking,
Nor supporting strength upon weakness.

CHORUS
Alas, can it be? Wert thou indeed   *Antistrophe 1*
Born into life with unseeing eyes?—a curst life,   150
A long life, so it must have been.
But a new curse shalt thou not
To old curses add today.
So halt there.
No further! nor intrude within
The silent depth of the grassy lawns
Of yonder glade where the bowl of pure

14

Water blends with the flowing stream
Of honey and milk. Beware then;   160
Have a care, unhappy stranger.
Depart—forth from the grove!—(A wide
Space yet parts us: he heeds us not.)
Do you hear, wandering way-worn wretch?
If there is aught you are wishing
To impart to us, quit that inviolate ground.
Where to all it is lawful,
There speak; but refrain in the meanwhile.

OEDIPUS
Daughter, what think you? How shall we answer?   170

ANTIGONE
O father, obey we must, and strive
To conform to the customs of this land.

OEDIPUS
Give me your hand then.

ANTIGONE
                        There, I have clasped yours.

OEDIPUS
Strangers, do me no injury, now that,
Trusting in you, I have left my refuge.

CHORUS
None, old man, shall attempt   *Strophe 2*
Forth from your place of safety against
Your will to compel you.

OEDIPUS
Yet further?

CHORUS
                Advance yet further.

OEDIPUS
Enough?

CHORUS
            Yet a few steps onward,   180
Maiden; for 'tis you must guide.

ANTIGONE

Follow me now, follow this way, father.
Dark your steps, but I lead you safely.

CHORUS

Learn, an alien on alien soil,
Poor wretch, learn to abhor whate'er
This city hates with a settled hate,
And that which it loves to reverence.

OEDIPUS

Then lead me, my child,
To a place where, entering lawful ground,
We may speak and listen unblamed, and so   190
Have done with warring against fate.

CHORUS

Stay now! Do not advance   *Antistrophe 2*
Further beyond that rocky floor
Shaped by no human hand.

OEDIPUS

Thus far?

CHORUS

          'Tis enough, I tell you.

OEDIPUS

Shall I sit?

CHORUS

          Yes, against the rock's edge
Crouch low. To your side it lies.

ANTIGONE

This is my task, dear father. Gently—

OEDIPUS

Woe! woe is me!

ANTIGONE

—A step, then another step—
Thus on your daughter's loving arm   200
Leaning firmly your aged limbs.

16

OEDIPUS
Woe for the doom of a dark soul!

CHORUS
Poor wretch, since you are now at ease,
Say: from whom are you sprung? Who are you
Miserably wandering thus? What soil
Gave you a home and fatherland?

OEDIPUS
O friends, I am cityless...but forbear...

CHORUS
What is it you would forbid, old man?

OEDIPUS
No, no! Who I am forbear to ask.   210
Seek not to learn; enquire no further.

CHORUS
What is this?

OEDIPUS
            Dread
Was my birth.

CHORUS
            Speak.

OEDIPUS
O my child, how
Shall I answer?

CHORUS
Come, say, who was your sire,
And the seed whence you were born.

OEDIPUS
What will become of me, child? Woe upon woe!

ANTIGONE
Better speak: you are forced to reveal it.

OEDIPUS
Then will I speak; for to hide it, no way is left.

CHORUS
We are tired of delay. Come, an answer!

OEDIPUS
To Laïus—know you?—a son...

CHORUS
Iou! Iou!   220

OEDIPUS
Of the Labdacid race was he...

CHORUS
                              O Zeus!

OEDIPUS
Oedipus, misery's child...

CHORUS
                                 So you are he?

OEDIPUS
Shudder not at the words I am uttering.

CHORUS
Io, O, O!

OEDIPUS
              Misery!

CHORUS
                       O, O!

OEDIPUS
What is now to befall us, my daughter?

CHORUS
Out with you straightway! Forth from the land both!

OEDIPUS
And your promise—how then will you keep that?

CHORUS
Never will fate punish one who requites
What another has done to him first.
The deceit of the one will but match the deceits   230
Of the other, and give
Never benefit, only revenge for reward.

18

So away with you! forth from the seats of the deities!
Out of my country begone with you, lest you should fasten
    upon
My city some heavier burden.

ANTIGONE
Strangers of wise, reverent soul,
Though the prayer of my aged sire
Might not appeal to you, since of his un-
purposed deeds you have heard the rumour,   240
Yet me at least, pity me the unfortunate,
Friends, I implore; since for naught
Else than my father alone do I plead with you,
Pleading with eyes yet unblinded, that so
I may look on your own as though truly a kinswoman
Sprung from the same blood as yours, that his misery
May find compassion. On you we depend
In our woe as it were on a god. But oh grant us
The grace that we scarce dare to hope.
By all to you nearest and dearest I implore you,   250
By wife or by children, by home or by deity.
Ne'er will you find any mortal man
Who, if a god lead him astray,
Yet could hope to escape doom.

LEADER OF CHORUS
Nay, child of Oedipus, we pity you
And him alike for your calamities;
But dreading the God's wrath, we dare not say
Aught beyond what already has been said.

OEDIPUS
Then what benefit comes of fair repute
And fame, if it must end in idle breath?
Since among cities Athens, so men say,   260
Is most god-fearing, and alone has power
To shelter and protect the afflicted exile—
Yet for me where's this shelter? From these rocks
You make me rise, then drive me from the land
Scared by my very name; not surely fearing

Me, nor my deeds; since all that I have done
Has been to suffer rather than to sin—
Were I to tell the true tale of my sire
And mother, for which you dread me—that full well
I know. Yet how by *nature* was I evil?   270
I did but requite wrong: so, had I acted
With knowledge, none even then could deem me wicked.
But all unknowing to my fate I went,
While they, who wronged me, sought my destruction
    knowingly.
Therefore, friend, I beseech you by the Gods:
You made me leave my refuge; then protect me.
Do not, while you pay honour to the Gods,
Refuse to do their bidding; but deem rather
That they regard alike the righteous man
And the unrighteous, so that never yet   280
For an impious mortal has escape been found.
Forbear therefore to cloud the glorious fame
Of Athens by a deed so impious;
But as you have received and pledged the suppliant,
So rescue and guard me to the end; nor scorn me
Beholding my unsightly countenance.
Sanctified by the Gods I come among you,
And I bring blessing to this folk. But when
The lord who is your ruler shall appear,
Then shall you hear and know all. And meanwhile   290
See to it that you treat me not unrighteously.

LEADER

Old man, we needs must listen with respect
To your remonstrance, which in no light words
You have uttered: and I am content to wait
Till the king of our land may judge thereof.

OEDIPUS

And where, friends, is the ruler of this country?

LEADER

Within his city: and the messenger
Who sent us hither, has gone to summon him.

OEDIPUS
Think you that for the blind man he will feel
Concern or esteem enough to come himself?   300

LEADER
Yes surely, so soon as he learns your name.

OEDIPUS
How will the rumour of my name reach him?

LEADER
The way is long enough for many rumours
To reach him. When he hears them, he will soon
Be with us, doubt not. For your name, old man,
Through every land has been so noised abroad
That even were he resting and loth to hasten,
Hearing of you, he will arrive with speed.

OEDIPUS
May his coming bless both me and his own city.
What generous man is not his own friend too?

ANTIGONE
O Zeus! can it be? What shall I think, father?   310

OEDIPUS
What is it, Antigone, my child?

ANTIGONE
                              A woman
I see coming towards us—mounted upon
A colt of Aetna—a Thessalian hat
She wears to screen her face from the sun's glare.
What shall I say?
Is it she, or is it not? Does fancy cheat me?
Yes, I am sure—but no—I cannot tell.
Ah dear soul!
It is no other. With bright smiling glances
She greets me as she draws near. It must be so: 320
Ismene herself it is, and no one else.

OEDIPUS
What say you, child?

21

ANTIGONE
                    I see your daughter here—
My sister. By her voice you soon shall know her.

Enter ISMENE.

ISMENE
Father and sister, of all names to me
Most sweet! How hardly have I found you at last!
And now scarce may I see you through my tears.

OEDIPUS
My child, you have come?

ISMENE
                    Father, I grieve to see you thus.

OEDIPUS
You are with me, child?

ISMENE
                    Yes, after long hardships.

OEDIPUS
Touch me, my daughter.

ISMENE
                    A hand to both of you.

OEDIPUS
Ah, children—sisters!

ISMENE
                    O most woeful life!   330

OEDIPUS
Her life and mine?

ISMENE
                    Mine too, the third in misery.

OEDIPUS
Child, why have you come?

ISMENE
                    Through care for you, dear father.

OEDIPUS
Longing to see me?

ISMENE   Yes; and to bring you tidings—
With the sole faithful servant that I had.

OEDIPUS
And the young men, your brothers—where are they?

ISMENE
They are—where they are. Fearful is now their plight.

OEDIPUS
How true an image of the ways of Egypt
Is shown by those two in their characters
And mode of life! For there within the house
The men sit weaving; but the wives, to earn   340
A livelihood abroad, go forth each day.
So in your case, my children, those to whom
Such toils are seemly, sit at home like girls,
While in their stead you bear for me my burden
Of miseries. One, soon as her tender age
Was past, and she had come to woman's strength,
Has ever been a guide to my old age
In my sad wanderings. Often through wild forests
Hungry and bare-foot she has roamed with me
Tormented by rainstorms and scorching suns,   350
Regretting not the comforts of a home
So but her father might be kindly tended.
(*Turning to* ISMENE) And you, child, often have you stolen
    away
From Thebes, bringing your father secretly
All the oracles that concerned him. A faithful watcher,
Since I was banished, for me have you been.
And now what further tidings have you brought,
Ismene? On what mission have you left home?
For well I know, you come not empty-handed,
Nor yet without some word of fear for me.   360

ISMENE
The sufferings I have borne, while far and wide
I sought the place where you were living, father,
Let me pass by. To recount all that misery,
And so endure it twice, there is no need.

But of the troubles that are threatening now
Your two unhappy sons, I am come to tell you.
Their first desire was that the throne be left
To Creon, and the city spared pollution,
When they considered how that ancient blight
Had cursed our race and clung to your sad home.   370
But now some god, or their own sinful mind,
Has stirred a wicked rivalry in these
Ill-fated men, to grasp at kingly power.
The impetuous youth, the younger born, has robbed
The elder, Polyneices, of the throne
And driven him outlawed from his fatherland.
But he, so it is rumoured, has now fled
To hill-girt Argos, and there found new kinsmen
By nuptial ties, and warriors for his friends,
Deeming that Argos will soon gloriously   380
Conquer the land of Thebes, or else, defeated,
Exalt her to the skies. No vain words, father,
Are these, but dreadful deeds. Would I might know
Where the Gods will have pity on your miseries.

OEDIPUS
What, have you then some hope that Heaven may still
Show pity and consent to my deliverance?

ISMENE
Yes, father, if these latest oracles...

OEDIPUS
What are they, child? And what do they foretell?

ISMENE
That by the Thebans for their welfare's sake
Alive or dead you shall yet be desired.   390

OEDIPUS
And to whom might good come from such as I?

ISMENE
On you, 'tis said, their power must depend.

OEDIPUS
So, when I am naught, then once more I am a man.

ISMENE
The Gods would lift you now whom once they crushed.

OEDIPUS
What mockery to lift age, when youth was ruined!

ISMENE
Well, be sure that on this account Creon
Will come to seek you, and rather soon than late.

OEDIPUS
Come with what purpose, daughter? Tell me plainly.

ISMENE
To plant you somewhere without the Theban borders,
Yet near enough to have you within their grasp.   400

OEDIPUS
What good can I do them from outside their borders?

ISMENE
For them your tomb neglected will be a curse.

OEDIPUS
It needs no oracle to teach us that.

ISMENE
Therefore they would acquire you as a neighbour
In some place where you'll not be your own master.

OEDIPUS
Will they also bury me in Theban earth?

ISMENE
No; guilt of a kinsman's blood allows not that.

OEDIPUS
Never shall the Cadmeäns be my masters.

ISMENE
Then someday shall this bring disaster upon them.

OEDIPUS
But how, my child, and where shall this befall?   410

ISMENE
Your wrath shall slay them embattled near your tomb.

OEDIPUS

And from whom heard you what you tell me, child?

ISMENE

From sacred envoys to the Delphian hearth.

OEDIPUS

Did Phoebus speak such things concerning me?

ISMENE

So say the men who have returned to Thebes.

OEDIPUS

Have my sons, either of them, heard of this?

ISMENE

Yes, both alike; and know it but too well.

OEDIPUS

Then those base men, aware of this, held kingship
More dear than the desire for my recall?

ISMENE

To hear your words grieves me; but I must bear them. 420

OEDIPUS

Then may the Gods seek not to reconcile
Their fated strife; and may it lie with me
To rule the issue of this war, which now
They are joining with spear lifted against spear.
For then neither should he abide who now
Holds sceptre and throne, nor should he that is banished
Ever return; since they did naught to help
Or defend me, their father, when so shamefully
I was thrust from my country; but stood by
When I was cast forth and proclaimed an exile. 430
In those days, you will say, by my own wish
The city with reason granted me that boon.
No, I say; no! for upon that first day,
When my soul still was seething, and when death,
Though it were by stoning, seemed most sweet to me,
There was none found to grant me that desire.
But afterwards, when all my misery
Was now assuaged, and I felt that my wrath

Had run too far in punishing those past sins,
Then, after all that time, then did the city   440
Fling me forth from the land, while they, my sons,
Who might have brought help to their sire, refused;
So I for lack of one small word from them
Must wander an outcast beggar for evermore.
It is these girls, my daughters, who provide
As best they may my daily sustenance,
Safe shelter, and the offices of kinship.
Those other two for a throne have sold their sire,
For sceptred despotism and tyranny.
But never shall they win me for their ally,   450
Nor from this lordship over Thebes shall good
Come to them: *that* I know, hearing these oracles
She brings, and meditating those old warnings
Spoken by Phoebus once, and here fulfilled.
Therefore let Creon, or whoever else
Bears rule in Thebes, be sent in quest of me;
Yet, friends, if you—with these dread Deities
Who dwell among your folk—consent to champion
And help me, a great deliverer shall you win
For Athens, and calamity for my foes.   460

LEADER OF CHORUS
Most worthy of compassion, Oedipus,
You and these maidens seem. And since you add
This promise to save Athens to your plea,
I would fain now advise you for your good.

OEDIPUS
Aid me, kind sir. I will obey you in all.

LEADER
Make now atonement to those Deities
To whose ground you first came, a trespasser.

OEDIPUS
But with what ceremonies? Instruct me, friends.

LEADER
First with clean hands from an ever-flowing fount
Holy drink-offerings hither must you bring.   470

27

OEDIPUS
And when I have gotten this pure draught, what then?

LEADER
Bowls are there, a cunning craftsman's handiwork.
Their edges and both handles you must crown.

OEDIPUS
With olive-sprays, with fillets, or how else?

LEADER
A ewe-lamb's fresh-shorn wool—that you must take.

OEDIPUS
I will. And then with what rite shall I end?

LEADER
With face turned to the dawn, drink-offerings pour.

OEDIPUS
And shall I pour them from those bowls you spoke of?

LEADER
Yes, in three streams; but empty the last bowl wholly.

OEDIPUS
With what am I to fill this vessel, tell me.   480

LEADER
With water and honey; but add to it no wine.

OEDIPUS
And when the grove's leaf-shadowed soil has drunk
    them...?

LEADER
Take thrice nine shoots of olive, and with both hands
Lay them upon the soil, and make this prayer.

OEDIPUS
How? in what words? That is what matters most.

LEADER
We call them the Benign Ones; and benignly
May they receive this suppliant who will save us.
That be your prayer, or theirs who pray for you—
A voiceless prayer: let no loud word be spoken.

Then retire, looking not behind. Thus do,   490
And I will dare to stand beside you boldly;
But else, stranger, I would have fears for you.

OEDIPUS
Daughters, you have heard these men who dwell near-by?

ANTIGONE
We have heard them. What now would you bid us do?

OEDIPUS
I cannot go. Doubly am I disabled:
I lack the strength; nor can I see my way.
Go then, one of you two; perform these rites;
Since surely for ten thousand one suffices
To make atonement, so there be good will.
But do with speed what must be done; nor leave me   500
Too long alone: for strength is no more mine
To walk unaided or with none to guide me.

ISMENE
Then will I go, and will perform this rite.
But first I would know where to find the place.

LEADER
On the grove's further side. Should you need help,
A guardian dwells near-by: he will direct you.

ISMENE
I go. But you, Antigone, stay here
And take good care of him. To protect a father
We must reck naught of toil, though toil there be.   *Exit.*

CHORUS
Cruel, stranger, it were to waken   *Strophe 1* 510
An old grief that has lain sleeping for long years;
Yet now do I yearn to hear it.

OEDIPUS
What mean you?

CHORUS
That dire grief, incurable and disastrous,
Wherewith you have wrestled vainly.

29

OEDIPUS
Uncover not, I beseech you,
Kind stranger, the shame I have suffered.

CHORUS
Since truly the tale is wide-spread and wanes not,
I am fain, friend, to hear from you now the whole truth.

OEDIPUS
Omoi!

CHORUS
Speak: let me entreat you.

OEDIPUS
No, no!

CHORUS
Consent; since all your requests by me were granted.   520

OEDIPUS
O kind friends, I have done deeds   *Antistrophe 1*
That have brought me anguish, unwitting deeds, as the
    Gods know,
Whereof not one was my own choice.

CHORUS
But how so?

OEDIPUS
I knew naught, naught, when in evil wedlock
Thebes bound me—a nuptial horror!

CHORUS
'Tis true then; you lay beside her,
Your mother—the bed polluting?

OEDIPUS
Omoi! they are cruel, cruel as death's self,
Such words. But these two, of me begotten...   530

CHORUS
What say you?

OEDIPUS
These, under a curse born...

CHORUS
O Zeus!

OEDIPUS
These two were born from the womb whose pangs
    bore me.

CHORUS
These then are at once your offspring, and...   *Strophe 2*

OEDIPUS
Their father's sisters of one womb born.

CHORUS
O horrible!

OEDIPUS   Horrible! Countless miseries,
Sweeping back upon my soul.

CHORUS
What agonies!

OEDIPUS
       Agonies dire to endure!

CHORUS
You sinned.

OEDIPUS
     Nay but I sinned not.

CHORUS
How so?

OEDIPUS
     A gift it was...
Wretch that I am, would that ne'er for delivering her   540
My city had bestowed such a gift upon me!

CHORUS
Unhappy man, so you shed the blood...   *Antistrophe 2*

OEDIPUS
What mean you? What do you seek to learn?

CHORUS
A father's blood?

OEDIPUS
            Ah me, a second
Blow you have smitten me, wound on wound.

CHORUS
You slew him?

OEDIPUS
            I slew him—but on my side...

CHORUS
What then?

OEDIPUS
      I had some justice.

CHORUS
How?

OEDIPUS
      I will tell you how.
They that I slew would as surely have murdered me.
Unwittingly into this sin did I fall without guilt.

LEADER OF CHORUS
See, at your summons, eager to learn your need
Theseus, our king, the son of Aegeus, comes.   550

Enter THESEUS.

THESEUS
Long have I known by hearsay, son of Laïus,
The cruel blinding of your eyes; and now
From such reports as reached me as I came hither
Surmise has grown to fuller certainty.
Your dress and your marred face reveal to me
Your name; and filled with pity I would ask you,
Ill-fated Oedipus, what is your suit
To Athens and to me, that you sit here,
You and the hapless maiden at your side.
Declare it. Dread indeed must be the tale   560
Of horror that could make me shrink from you—
Me, who was reared in exile, like yourself,

32

And in strange lands at hazard of my life
Wrestled with perils, as no man beside.
Never then would I turn from or refuse
Aid to a homeless stranger, such as you.
Being mortal, I know well that in the morrow
My portion is no greater than your own.

OEDIPUS
Theseus, your nobleness in brief words has shown
That for me there is need to say but little.   570
Who I am, from what father I was born,
From what land I have come, you have rightly said.
And so naught else but to speak my desire
Remains for me—and the whole tale is told.

THESEUS
Make known to me your desire. I long to hear it.

OEDIPUS
I come to offer you my woe-worn body,
A gift that is not comely to behold;
Yet the gains from it far exceed mere beauty.

THESEUS
And what gain do you claim to have brought with you?

OEDIPUS
Hereafter you shall learn that, but not now.   580

THESEUS
But say, when will your benefit be revealed?

OEDIPUS
When I am dead, and you have given me burial.

THESEUS
You ask for life's last boon; for all between
You seem to take no thought, or to care nothing.

OEDIPUS
Yes, for I gain all else by that one boon.

THESEUS
Then small of compass is the grace you crave.

OEDIPUS
Yet give heed. No light issue verily is this.

THESEUS
Do you mean strife betwixt your sons and me?

OEDIPUS
King, they intend to carry me hence to Thebes.

THESEUS
If you consent, exile is no more seemly.   590

OEDIPUS
Yes; but when I was willing, they refused.

THESEUS
O folly! Wrath in ill-fortune is not meet.

OEDIPUS
When you have heard me, chide; till then forbear.

THESEUS
Say on. I must not blame you without knowledge.

OEDIPUS
I have suffered, Theseus, cruel wrong on wrong.

THESEUS
You mean that ancient trouble of your race?

OEDIPUS
No: *that* is noised abroad through all the Hellenes.

THESEUS
What grief is this, passing the griefs of men?

OEDIPUS
Thus it is: from my country have I been driven
By my own offspring; and to return no more,   600
As one who slew his father, is my doom.

THESEUS
How should they fetch you, if you must dwell in exile?

OEDIPUS
By the God's oracle they will be compelled.

34

THESEUS
What prophecy of disaster do they fear?

OEDIPUS
That in this land they some day must be conquered.

THESEUS
How between them and me should discord come?

OEDIPUS
Dear son of Aegeus, to the Gods alone
Old age and death come never; but all else
Time, that is lord of all things, shall dissolve.
Earth's strength decays, and the strength of the body;   610
Trust between men dies, and distrust is born;
And among friends or between city and city
Never for long does the same spirit blow.
For, be it soon or late, men find that sweet
Changes to bitter, and once more to friendship.
And though all is fair weather now between
Your city and Thebes, yet Time's unnumbered lapse
Gives birth to unnumbered nights and days, wherein
They shall dissolve and sunder with the spear
Today's pledged concord for some trivial cause;   620
When, in the cold tomb slumbering, my corpse
Shall one day drink their warm blood, if Zeus still
Be Zeus, and Phoebus, son of Zeus, speak true.
But these are mysteries I must not utter;
So let me end with my first prayer. This only:
Make your word good, and never shall you say
That in vain you welcomed Oedipus to dwell
Here in your land—if the Gods spoke not false.

LEADER
King, from the first this man has shown the wish,
As he has promised, so to bless our land.   630

THESEUS
Who would reject friendship from such a man?
Since to him, first, the hearth of an ally
Is always open mutually between us;
Next, as a suppliant to our Gods he comes,

35

Bringing great benefits to this land and me.
Therefore I honour him, nor spurn his grace,
But stablish him a citizen in our realm.
And if he would abide here, in your charge
I leave him; or would he rather come with me—
The choice is yours, Oedipus: whatsoever   640
To you seems best, your will shall be my own.

OEDIPUS
Zeus, worthily mayst thou recompense such men.

THESEUS
What would you then? To my house would you come?

OEDIPUS
Yes, were that lawful: but here in this place...

THESEUS
What then will you do here? I will not thwart you.

OEDIPUS
Here shall I vanquish those who banished me.

THESEUS
Great good you promise from your sojourn here.

OEDIPUS
Yes, if you keep with me your plighted word.

THESEUS
Put faith in me: never will I betray you.

OEDIPUS
With an oath I will not bind you, whom I trust.   650

THESEUS
Well, you would gain no more than by my word.

OEDIPUS
How then will you act?

THESEUS
                    What may it be you fear?

OEDIPUS
There will come men...

THESEUS
                    Nay, these will look to that.

OEDIPUS
Yet, should you leave me...

THESEUS
                              Teach me not my duty.

OEDIPUS
Fear constrains me...

THESEUS
                    My heart feels no fear.

OEDIPUS
You know not what they threaten.

THESEUS
                              This I know,
That none in my despite shall take you hence.
Many the threatenings, many the loud vain words
That men fling out in wrath; but when the mind
Masters itself once more, the threats are gone.   660
And though these may have dared utter dread boasts
How they will hale you hence, yet shall they find
The sundering waters wide and hard to sail.
Take courage then, apart from my resolve
To aid you, if it be Phoebus sent you hither.
Still, though I be not present, I know well
That my name from all outrage will protect you.

Exit THESEUS.

CHORUS
To a land, stranger, of noble horses,   *Strophe 1*
The fairest of earth's abodes thou comest,
To white-gleaming Colonus, where   670
Nightingales ever love to haunt
Trilling loudly their liquid carols
Hidden close in the green groves,
Dwelling midst of the wine-dark ivy,
The God's bower inviolate
Rich with a myriad fruits and unvisited
By sun, where never fierce storms
Of wind bluster, and where the reveller
Dionysus is ever wont to wander
Companioned by the Nymphs that nursed him.   680

37

And there, wet with the dew of heaven,   *Antistrophe 1*
Narcissus in lovely clusters morn by
Morn is blooming, the ancient crown
Of those great Goddesses; there the yellow
Sheen of crocus; and there in sleepless
Never minishing streams and rills
Kephisus spreadeth his vagrant waters;
And each day with his unstained flood
Over the plains of the land's swelling bosom
He moveth, ever bestowing   690
Quick fertility—haunts frequented
By quires of the Muses and the golden-
reined chariot of Aphrodite.

Also a wonder there is   *Strophe 2*
Whereof the like never has fame told me,
Whether on Asian soil risen to the light,
Or on the great Dorian isle of Pelops—
A scion undestroyable, self-renewing,
A terror to invading spearmen:
For in this land mightily doth flourish   700
The gray-leafed olive tree, nurturer of children;
And no man, be he youthful, or be he aged,
Shall with ravaging hand dare to destroy it; for the
      ever-watchful glance
Of Morian Zeus and flashing-eyed
Athena behold and guard it.

Now yet another praise   *Antistrophe 2*
Have I to tell for this our mother city,
That proud gift of the great bountiful God,
Noblest of all glories our land may boast,   710
The might of the horse, the might of the young colt,
The might of the sea: for thus in pride
Thou hast throned her, O son of Cronos, King Poseidon;
Since in these roads first thou didst reveal
The curb's power that tames the unruly stallion.
Also the smooth oar, shaped to the hand, with wondrous
      speed

Leaps following from wave to wave
The hundred feet of the Nereids.

ANTIGONE
O Land so nobly praised, now is the time   720
To make those bright praises shine forth in deeds.

OEDIPUS
Child, what new danger do you see?

ANTIGONE
                                    Creon
Draws near to us, father—followed by armed men.

OEDIPUS
Befriend me now, kind elders. You alone
Can give me final safety from my foes.

LEADER
Fear not: it shall be yours. Though I be aged,
Yet the strength of this land has not grown old.

Enter CREON *with* ATTENDANTS.

CREON
Sirs—nobly-born dwellers in this land,
I see that with a sudden fear your eyes
Are troubled at my coming: but from me   730
Shrink not, nor to ungentle words give voice.
For with no thought of force I come, being old,
And knowing that the town whereto I am come
Is mighty, if any town is mighty in Hellas.
But, in my old age, I am sent to plead
With this man, that he return with me to Thebes;
Nor am I one man's envoy, but so charged
By all our people; since, as his kinsman, I
More than all others must lament his sufferings.
But listen, unhappy Oedipus; consent   740
And come home. Rightfully the whole Theban folk
Summons you; and most rightfully do I,
Since, if I be not basest of all men born,
It is I who grieve most for your griefs, old man,

When I behold you thus a wretched stranger
And vagrant, ever roaming in penury,
With this one handmaid. Alas, I had not thought
That she would fall to such a depth of misery
As this whereto she has fallen, unhappy girl,
Evermore with a beggar's sustenance   750
Comforting your blind life—so young, but still
Unwed, a prey for the first hand to snatch.
Ah cruel is the reproach that I have cast
Against thee, against me, and all our race.
But such clear shame cannot be hid; then by
Thy fathers' gods, Oedipus, hide it thou,
Consenting to return to thine own city
And house, with kindly farewell to this State,
For she is worthy: yet thy home, that of old
Nurtured thee, has the first right to thy reverence.   760

OEDIPUS
O shameless villain, who from any plea
Of justice would derive some cunning wile,
Why do you thus tempt me and seek once more
To take me in toils where capture would most grieve me?
For first, when, tortured by my self-wrought woes,
Gladly had I been cast forth from the land,
You then would not consent to grant that boon:
But when my anguish had now spent itself,
And to abide within the house was sweet,
Then would you banish and drive me forth, nor then   770
For kinship had you any care at all.
And now again, seeing me kindly welcomed
By this land and by all her sons, you seek
To snatch me away with hard words that seem soft.
What joy is in kindness done against our will?
If a man should refuse to succour you
When you besought him for his aid, but after
Your soul's desire had been sated, then
Should grant it, when the grace was no more gracious,
Would you not find that pleasure to be vain?   780
Yet such are the offers that you make to me:

Though good in words, in substance they are evil.
Now to these men will I reveal your falseness.
You have come, not to fetch me home, but near
Your own borders to plant me, that your city
May be unscathed by troubles from this land.
That portion is not for you, but *this*: my curse
Upon your country, ever abiding there;
And for my sons this heritage, enough room
Within my land to die there, and no more.   790
As for the fate of Thebes, am I not wiser
Than you by far, since more true is my knowledge,
From Phoebus and his father, Zeus himself?
But you come hither with a tongue suborned,
Tempered like hard steel; yet you are more like
To win defeat than safety by your pleading.
But of this never shall I persuade you. Go then;
Allow us to live here. Not even this life
Is evil, so therewith we are content.

CREON
Which, think you, suffers most in this dispute,   800
I by your folly, or you by your self-will?

OEDIPUS
I shall be satisfied if your pleading fails
Both with myself and with these citizens.

CREON
Unhappy man, to whom years bring not wisdom,
How you disgrace old age by living on!

OEDIPUS
You are ready of tongue: but never have I known
Honest men who spoke well for every cause.

CREON
One may speak many words yet miss one's aim.

OEDIPUS
Your words no doubt were few yet aimed aright.

CREON
No, not for one whose wits are such as yours.   810

OEDIPUS

Depart—for these men too I speak—beset not
This haven where I am destined to abide.

CREON

To these men, not to you, I appeal. But since
You insult your kindred thus, once I have seized you...

OEDIPUS

And who could seize me with such friends to protect me?

CREON

Yet, even so, with grief you shall be pierced.

OEDIPUS

Where is the deed which warrants such a threat?

CREON

Of your two daughters one have I seized already
And sent to Thebes; this other will I now take.

OEDIPUS

Woe's me!

CREON

Soon will you have more woe to endure.   820

OEDIPUS

You have stolen my child?

CREON

And will have this one soon.

OEDIPUS

Ah, friends, what will you do? Will you forsake me?
Nay drive this godless robber from your land.

LEADER

Begone, stranger, forthwith! Wicked the deed
You have done; wicked is that you threaten now.

CREON *to his* ATTENDANTS

'Tis time for you to lead this girl away
By force, unless she come of her own will.

ANTIGONE

Oh horrible! whither shall I fly? oh where
Find help from Gods or men?

42

LEADER
Forbear, stranger!

CREON
That man I will not touch—but her who is mine.   830

OEDIPUS
Help, good elders!

LEADER
This deed, Sir, is not just.

CREON
It *is* just.

LEADER
How?

CREON
I take what is my own.

OEDIPUS
O city of Athens!   *Strophe*

CHORUS
Beware man! Release this maid, or it will soon
Come to the test of blows.

CREON
Stand back!

CHORUS
Not from you,
If you attempt this crime.

CREON
It will be war with Thebes, if you should injure me.

OEDIPUS
Did I not warn you it would be war?

CHORUS
Unhand the maid
At once, I say.

CREON
Command not where you are not master.

CHORUS
Leave hold, I tell you.

CREON *to* ATTENDANTS

Come now, take her, and begone. 840

CHORUS
Oh haste, men of Colonus! hasten hither to aid!
The city is wronged—my city—threatened by violent men.
Oh haste, haste to my side.

ANTIGONE
They are dragging me away. Ah friends, my friends!

OEDIPUS
Where art thou, daughter?

ANTIGONE

I am borne along by force.

OEDIPUS
Thy hands, my child—where, where?

ANTIGONE

Nay, I am helpless.

CREON
Come, take her hence.

OEDIPUS

Oh misery, misery!

Exeunt attendants with ANTIGONE.

CREON
So never again shall those two crutches prop
Your wandering steps. But since it is your will
To defeat your country and your friends (who bade me   850
Perform this duty, though a prince), be then
That victory yours. The day will surely come
When you will learn that now, as in time past,
You have done yourself no good, when, spite of friends,
You indulged anger, that ever has been your bane.

LEADER
Hold, stranger, hold!

CREON

You dare lay hands on me!

LEADER
You shall not go till you give back these maidens.

CREON
Then a still dearer prize soon shall you forfeit
To Thebes. Not only these two girls will I seize.

LEADER
What mean you?

CREON   This man too will I take with me.   860

LEADER
A brave threat!

CREON   Straightway shall it be fulfilled.

LEADER
Unless the ruler of our land prevent you.

OEDIPUS
Oh shameless menace! Will you dare to touch me?

CREON
Keep silence.

OEDIPUS   No—but may these Deities
Suffer me yet to give voice to this curse.
Ah villain, who by force hast robbed my blindness
Of that defenceless eye that lent me sight!
Therefore both on thyself and on thy kindred
May the God who sees all things, the Sun-god,
Inflict an old age such as mine has been.   870

CREON
Hear you this wickedness, people of the land?

OEDIPUS
They hear both me and thee, and know my wrongs
Are deeds, and my revenge is naught but words.

CREON
I will not curb my wrath. Alone though I be,
And slow with age, by force will I capture him.

OEDIPUS
Oh misery!   *Antistrophe*

CHORUS
A bold spirit is yours to dare such a deed.
Verily your hope is vain.

CREON
How vain?

CHORUS
            Else would I deem
Athens a city no more.

CREON
In a just cause the feeble vanquishes the strong.   880

OEDIPUS
Hear you his words?

CHORUS
                Words that he shall not turn to deeds,
Zeus be my witness!

CREON
                Zeus alone knows that, not you.

CHORUS
What insolence!

CREON
                Yes, insolence which you must bear.

CHORUS
Oh hear, citizens all! Oh hear, chieftains, hear!
Hither without delay! Hither! Across our borders
The foe fain would flee.

Enter THESEUS.

THESEUS
What is this outcry? What this tumult? By what fear
    are you possessed,
Thus at the altar of the Sea-god to interrupt my sacrifice
To the Lord of your Colonus? Speak: the whole truth I
    would know:
Why have I been compelled to hasten hither with such
    unwelcome speed?   890

46

OEDIPUS

O dearest friend—for well do I know your voice—
This man but now has done me cruel wrong.

THESEUS

What is that wrong? Who has done you injury?

OEDIPUS

Creon, whom here you see, has snatched my two
Sole children, and would hale them from your land.

THESEUS
What do you tell me?

OEDIPUS   Now you have heard my wrong.

THESEUS
Let one of my attendants run to the altars
With all speed, and command the assembled folk
To leave the sacrifice and haste together,
Footmen, and horsemen galloping with slack rein,   900
To the place where the two roads meet; that so
These maidens may not pass there, and I, thus robbed
By force, become a mockery to this stranger.
Go, I bid you—go quickly. (*Turning towards* CREON)
    But this man,
If my wrath went as far as he deserves,
Should not escape unpunished from my hand.
Now by such law as he himself has brought,
And by no other, must he be convicted.
You shall not leave this land until you bring
Those maidens hither and set them in my sight.   910
For your deed has laid shame upon myself,
Upon your country and your ancestors.
To a justice-loving land you come, that sanctions
No lawless deed; yet you have swept aside
Her lawful powers, entering thus with violence,
Seizing and carrying captive what you will;
As though you deemed my city empty of men,
Or manned by slaves, and me a thing of naught.
Yet not by Theban training are you base.
Thebes is not wont to rear unrighteous men.   920

47

Nor would she praise you if she learnt your acts
Of robbery against me, against the Gods,
Whose wretched suppliants you would rape by force.
If it were I had set foot on *your* land,
Though of all claims my claim were the most just,
Never would I without leave of your ruler
Plunder or drag away; but I should know
How an alien should live mid citizens.
But your own city, that deserves it not,
You are shaming; and the fulness of your years   930
Has brought you an old age bereft of wisdom.
I have said then, and I say it once again:
Hither with all speed let those girls be brought,
Unless you'ld be a sojourner in this land
By force, against your will. These words my lips
Have uttered, speak the purpose of my soul.

LEADER
Is this so, stranger? From a righteous race
You are said to come; but your words are found evil.

CREON
Son of Aegeus, not because I thought this city
Void, as you said, of manhood, nor of counsel,   940
Have I thus acted; but because I deemed
That this people could never so well love
My kinsfolk as against my will to foster them.
Moreover I felt sure they would not welcome
A parricide, a polluted man, whose parent
Had been the unholy bride of her own son.
Such wisdom dwells, I knew, within their land
Upon the Mount of Ares, which denies
Harbourage in this city to such outcasts.
In that faith did I seek to take this prize: 950
Nor had I done so, had he not invoked
Bitter curses on me and on my race.
To me, thus wronged, this requital seemed just.
For wrath knows no old age, until we come
To die. Only the dead feel no affront.
Act therefore as to you seems good; for though

48

The words I speak be just, through lack of aid
I am feeble. None the less, old though I be,
I will endeavour to meet deed with deed.

O shameless arrogance! This taunt, where think you   960
Does it fall—on my age, or on your own?
Bloodshed, incest, disasters have your lips
Shot forth against me—miseries I have not willed
But endured. Such was the pleasure of the Gods,
Wroth with our race, it may be, from of old.
No guilt to upbraid me with could you discover
In me alone, guilt which should drive me thus
To sin against myself, against my kin.
For tell me, though some god-sent oracle
Had doomed my father by a son's hand to die,   970
How with that guilt could you reproach me justly,
Whom no sire had begotten yet, no mother
Had yet conceived—but I was then unborn?
And if, being born, as I was, to misfortune,
Meeting my father, I fought with him and slew him,
Ignorant what I was doing, and to whom,
How could you justly blame the unwitting crime?
And will you force me, shameless wretch, to speak
Of your own sister's nuptials—of my mother's?
Hear then; for now no more will I be silent,   980
Now that in impious speech you have gone so far.
For she had borne me, had borne me—ah woeful fate!
I knew it not, nor she—and, for her shame,
To me, whom she had borne, she bare children.
But this I know: your will consents to slander
Both her and me; but I willed not to wed her;
And not of my free will do I speak now.
   But neither in this marriage can I be called
Guilty, nor in that slaying of my father
Whereof you accuse me with such bitter taunts.   990
Answer but this one question: if here and now
Someone were to assault you and seek to slay you,
The just man, would you ask that murderer,

Was he your father? or straightway would you smite him?
Surely, as you love your life, you would requite
The culprit, nor look round you to find your warrant.
But such the plight whereto, led by the Gods,
I came. And could my sire return to life,
In this, sure am I, he would not gainsay me.
Yet you—who are no just man, who know no difference   1000
Between what should be spoken and what should not—
You before these men revile me thus.
You find it timely to flatter the fame of Theseus,
And praise Athens for her well-ordered state;
Yet this for all your praises you forget:
That in wise knowledge how to pay due worship
To the just Gods, this land excels all others;
Whence you would steal me, an aged suppliant,
Having first seized and haled away my daughters.
Therefore now on these Goddesses I call,   1010
I supplicate and adjure them to bring help
And fight upon my side, that you may learn
By what manner of men this city is guarded.

LEADER
O King, the stranger is worthy of our succour.
Though a curse be upon him he is innocent.

THESEUS
Enough of words. They who have done this wrong
Are in flight; we, whom they have wronged, stand idle.

CREON
I am in your power. What would you have me do?

THESEUS
Show me the way. I will escort you; and so,
If near this place you are holding the girls captive,   1020
You may yourself discover them to me.
But if your men are fleeing with the spoil,
Then others will pursue them: from this land
Never shall they escape to thank their gods.
Lead on. See how the robber has been robbed;
How Fate has taken the hunter in the toils.

Soon lost are prizes won by wicked guile.
You shall have none to abet you here. I know
You have accomplices, else had you never
Found courage for this outrage. There was someone   1030
In whom you trusted to aid you in this crime.
And to this I must look with heed, nor suffer
My city to be weaker than one man.
Do you take my drift? or seem these warnings vain,
As seemed those, when you were plotting your misdeeds?

CREON
While we are here, say what you will unchallenged.
But I too, at home, will know how I must act.

THESEUS
Threaten now, but set forth. You, Oedipus,
Stay here in peace, relying on my pledge
That, if I die not first, I will not rest   1040
Until I have restored to you your children.

OEDIPUS
Heaven bless you, Theseus, for your noble heart,
And for your righteous zeal to succour me.

Exeunt THESEUS, CREON, *and* ATTENDANTS.

CHORUS
Oh would that I now might be   *Strophe 1*
Where the foe, soon brought to bay,
Will join battle with clash of bronze,
Whether on the Pythian shore, or by that torch-lit strand
Where the Goddesses reveal
Dread mysteries to mortals, on whose lips   1050
The Hierophant has laid
The golden seal of silence:
For there, amid the war-cry of the rescuers,
Within our borders shall the valiant Theseus
Deliver the sister maidens.

Or perchance over the pastures   *Antistrophe 1*
Westward of Oea's snowy rocks,   1060

51

On horses or racing chariots
In their flight will they be speeding.
It is he who will be vanquished.
Terrible are our warriors, and terrible
Is the might of the men of Theseus.
Every bit and bridle flashes;
With slack rein swiftly gallops every horseman   1070
Who worships Athena
That lover of horse and rider,
And the earth-girdling Sea-god,
The beloved son of Rhea.

Now are they fighting—or not yet?   *Strophe 2*
For with strong hope my soul
Woos me that I may soon
Behold the maidens wronged so sorely,
Outraged by a kinsman's hand.
Today, today Zeus will work some great thing.
Victory my soul presages.   1080
Would that I were a dove with the swift strength
Of a storm, that I might soar to an airy cloudland,
Thence to gaze downward upon the combat.

Oh hear, all ruling lord of Gods,   *Antistrophe 2*
All-seeing Zeus! Unto the guardians
Of this land grant thou to achieve
Victoriously pursuit and rescue
Till the prize be found and won.
Thou too, divine Pallas Athene—   1090
And the hunter Apollo, and she his sister,
Follower of the dappled deer's swift flight,
Oh may they both come hither as mighty champions
Of this land of Athens and her people.

LEADER
Friend wanderer, you have no need to tax
Your watcher with false augury; for yonder
The maidens are drawing near amid their escort.

Enter THESEUS *with* ANTIGONE *and* ISMENE.

OEDIPUS
Where—where? What say you?

ANTIGONE
O father, father!
Might but some God give thee sight to behold   1100
This best of men who has brought us here to thee!

OEDIPUS
My child, you are both here?

ANTIGONE
Yes, these strong arms
Have saved us—Theseus and his trusty warriors.

OEDIPUS
Come hither, children; come to your father's arms.
Let me embrace you, beyond hope restored.

ANTIGONE
Your longing shall be granted: we too crave it.

OEDIPUS
Where are you—where?

ANTIGONE
We are coming, both together.

OEDIPUS
Ah dearest children!

ANTIGONE
A father loves his own.

OEDIPUS
Props of my age!

ANTIGONE
And sharers of your misery.

OEDIPUS
I hold my dear ones. Since you have come to me,   1110
Though now I died, I were not wholly woeful.
Press close to me on this side and on that;
Cling to your father, children, and repose
From all these desolate unhappy wanderings.
But now, as shortly as you may, tell me
How it befell: brief speech becomes young maidens.

ANTIGONE

Here is our rescuer. He must tell you all,
Since his the deed: so shall my part be brief.

OEDIPUS

Friend, marvel not, if to my girls, restored
Beyond hope, I prolong my talk thus eagerly.   1120
For well I know, this joy at their return
Has come to me from thee, and thee alone.
For thou, and no man else, hast rescued them.
So may the Gods reward thee and this land
According to my wish: for among you
Alone of mortals have I found the fear
Of Heaven, and equity, and lips that lie not.
Knowing this, I requite you with these praises;
For what I have, I have through thee, thee only.
Now, King, stretch forth your hand, that I may touch it;   1130
And, if it be lawful, let me kiss your face.—
But what am I asking? How should a wretch like me
Wish you to touch one with whom every stain
Of sin has made its home? Not *that* will I ask,
Nay nor allow you. They alone can share
This burden, who have experience of such woe.
Take my blessing there where you stand, and still
With loyal zeal protect me, as till this hour.

THESEUS

That lovingly and lengthily in your joy
You have spoken with your children, I marvel not;   1140
Nor that you first should heed *their* words, not mine.
Indeed there is naught that should offend me in that.
'Tis not through words, but through the deeds I do,
That I would make my life illustrious!
I have given proof. In what I promised you,
Old man, I have not failed. I am come, and with me
Your daughters, living, and by those threats unharmed.
And how the fight was won, what need to boast
Idly? From them at leisure you will learn it.

But there was a strange rumour I heard just now   1150
As I came hither: thereon I need your counsel;

54

For small though it seem, it moves me to some wonder:
And a mortal should deem nothing beneath his care.

OEDIPUS
What is it, son of Aegeus? Tell me now;
For I know naught of that whereof you enquire.

THESEUS
A man, they say—no countryman of yours,
But of your kin—has cast himself a suppliant
At the altar of Poseidon, where, before
I first came hither, I was offering sacrifice.

OEDIPUS
From what land came he? And wherefore a suppliant?   1160

THESEUS
This only I know: brief speech with you he asks,
But such, they say, as need not harass you.

OEDIPUS
On what theme? A suppliant's prayer is no light matter.

THESEUS
He asks no more than to confer with you,
Then to return safe from his journey hither.

OEDIPUS
Who can he be, this suppliant who sits there?

THESEUS
Is there perchance some kinsman of yours who dwells
At Argos, who might crave this boon of you?

OEDIPUS
Ah friend, say no word more.

THESEUS   Why, what ails you?

OEDIPUS
Ask not this thing of me.

THESEUS
                    Ask what?—Speak.   1170

OEDIPUS
By those words I know well who is the suppliant.

55

THESEUS
Who can he be, that I must needs condemn him?

OEDIPUS
My son, O King—a son I hate, whose voice
Would vex me as the voice of no man else.

THESEUS
What? Surely you can listen, yet not act
Against your will. Why were it pain to hear him?

OEDIPUS
Most hateful to his father has become
That voice. Constrain me not to yield in this.

THESEUS
Beware; does not his suppliant state constrain you?
To the God you owe this duty of respect.   1180

ANTIGONE
Father, let me persuade you, young though I be.
Allow the King to content his own heart,
And to content the God, as he desires.
Yield to your daughters: let our brother come.
Fear not lest he pluck you from your resolve
By words that are not spoken for your good.
What harm can come of listening? Deeds designed
With evil purpose, by speech are betrayed.
You gave him birth. Even were he to wrong you
With the most impious wickedness, my father,   1190
For you to pay back wrong cannot be lawful.
Let him come. Others too have evil offspring.
Though swift to wrath, they heed the advice of friends,
Charmed by whose spells their nature is subdued.
Look to the past, not to the present: ponder
On all those woes you have borne through sire and
       mother.
Thus pondering, sure I am, you will discern
How wrath is evil and hath an evil end.
Good reason have you so to meditate,
Thus bereft of your eyes, for ever sightless.   1200

Ah, yield. It is not seemly that just suitors
Should sue for long, or that a man should meet
With kindness, yet lack good will to requite it.

OEDIPUS
Child, grievous is this favour which your pleading
Wins from me.—Well then, as you will, so be it.
(*To* THESEUS.) Only, friend, if that man is to come hither,
Let no one become master of my life.

THESEUS
There was no need to ask that of me twice,
Old man. I would not boast; but rest assured,
Your freedom is safe, while any God saves mine. *Exit.*   1210

CHORUS
Whoso yearns for an ampler portion   *Strophe*
Of life, scorning a modest span,
Naught of him can I truly deem
Save that his heart is possessed by folly.
For long days will be storing up
Many a memory nearer far
To grief. As for thy dear delights,
Where, oh where are they gone today,
When life beyond the fitting term
Now is lapsing, and the deliverer
Cometh to each man,   1220
When on a sudden his doom is revealed
Without song hymenaeal or music of chorus
And lyre, even death that ends all.

Not to be born is of mortal fates   *Antistrophe*
The best; but when he hath seen the light
The next best will it be, thither
Whence he hath come to return with all speed.
For when once he has seen that youth
Has passed by with its idle dreams,   1230
With what woes will he now be vexed,
With what labour and weariness—
With envy, faction, discord, strife,
Wars and bloodshed? Then as a last plague

He falleth a victim
To friendless unsociable weak unregarded
Scorned old age, in whose company naught but
Sorrow on sorrow dwelleth.

In such plight is yon poor wretch, not I alone.   *Epode*
As some rocky cape that fronts the north wind   1240
Lashed by the fierce storm-driven waves from all sides,
So he too by the dire woes
Wave-like over him breaking
Is lashed savagely ever without a respite,
Some from the westerly sinking sun,
Some from his eastern chambers,
Some from his noon's glory,
Some down from the peaks of the gloomed North.

ANTIGONE
See yonder, that is the suppliant: alone
Without attendants he is coming, father.   1250
Down from his eyes tears are streaming fast.

OEDIPUS
Who is this man?

ANTIGONE
                    The same who from the first
Was in our thoughts—Polyneices stands before you.

Enter POLYNEICES.

POLYNEICES
Oimoi, what shall I do? Shall I first weep
For my own sorrows, or for my aged father's?
Whom I have found here in a foreign land
In exile with you two, my sisters, clothed
In such raiment, whereof the loathsome squalor
Has clung so long upon his ancient form,
Blighting his flesh, while over the sightless eyes   1260
His unkempt hair falls fluttering in the breeze.
And a like sign of misery is the wallet
Wherein he carries food to stay his hunger.
Ah wretch accurst! all this too late I learn.

Thus am I proved by such neglect of thee
Most vile: my own lips witness what I am.
But since, in all he does, Zeus summons Mercy
To share his throne, at thy side also, father,
May she now stand; for these offences might
Perchance be healed, but never be made worse.　　　1270
Why are you silent?—
Speak, father—one word. Turn not away from me.
No answer? Nothing? Will you in mute contempt
Dismiss me, with no word of why you are wroth?
Oh you, who are his children, and my sisters,
Endeavour, you at least, to move our father's
Unapproachable, inexorable silence.
Let him not send me away dishonoured—me
The suppliant of a God—without response.

ANTIGONE
Yourself tell him your need, unhappy brother.　　　1280
Words as they flow will often touch the heart,
Or glow with indignation or with pity,
And so will somehow give to the dumb a voice.

POLYNEICES
Wise is your counsel. Boldly will I speak.
First to the God himself I appeal for help,
Since from his altar the sovereign of this land
Bade me arise and gave me leave to speak
And take my answer, then depart unharmed.
I entreat you, strangers, may this pledge be honoured
By you, and by my sisters, and my sire.　　　1290
　But now will I tell you, father, why I came.
I have been driven from my fatherland
A banished man, because, as eldest-born,
I claimed your sovereign throne. But Eteocles,
The younger, thrust me from the land, though neither
In argument had he worsted me, nor dared
Trial by combat, but had somehow won
The city over. And of this I deem
The Fury of your house is the chief cause.
So too by soothsayers have I heard it said.　　　1300

But when I came to Dorian Argos, there
I took to wife the daughter of Adrastus,
And bound to me by oath all of that land
Who are deemed the foremost in renown of war,
That with them levying seven bands of spearmen
Against Thebes, I might die in a just cause,
Or from the realm cast him who had done that wrong.
Well, but why then have I come hither now?
To thee, father, I come with suppliant prayers,
My own, and those of my allies, who now,   1310
With seven spears leading their seven hosts,
Around the walls of Thebes have set their leaguer.
The first is Amphiaraüs, matchless in skill
To fling the spear, matchless in augury;
The second, Oeneus' son, Aetolian Tydeus;
Eteoclus the third, of Argive birth;
The fourth, Hippomedon, sent by his father
Talaos; the fifth is Capaneus, who vaunts
That he will burn Thebes to the ground with fire;
The sixth, Arcadian Parthenopaeus, named   1320
From that virgin of other days, who bare him
In wedlock, Atalanta's trusty son.
Last I, thy son (or if not thine, but offspring
Of evil fate, yet thine at least in name),
Lead the brave host of Argos against Thebes.
   By these your daughters, father, and by your life,
We all pray and implore you to remit
Your heavy wrath against me, as I go forth
To wreak vengeance against my brother, who thus
Has thrust me out and robbed me of my birth-land.   1330
For if the truth is told by oracles,
Victory will be with those whom you shall aid.
Then by our fountains, by our native Gods,
I entreat you to hearken and to yield.
An exiled beggar am I, an exile thou;
Only by courting others have we a home,
Both you and I; we are sharers of one doom;
While he, king in the palace—woe is me!—
Mocks in his pride at both of us alike.

But if you assist my purpose, with small toil   1340
And in brief time will I destroy his tyranny.
So in your own house will I stablish you,
And myself also, casting him out by force.
Thus may I boast, if you consent herein:
Without you, I cannot even return alive.

LEADER
For his sake who has sent him, Oedipus,
Speak as seems wise, ere you dismiss the man.

OEDIPUS
Nay then, you who are guardians of this land,
Were it not Theseus who has sent him hither,
Judging it right that he should hear my answer,   1350
Never would he have hearkened to my voice.
But now he shall be favoured, ere he go,
Hearing such words as shall not gladden his soul.
(*Turning on* POLYNEICES) Villain, when you possessed
        the sceptre and throne
Of Thebes, where now your brother reigns, you drove me,
Your father, into banishment, and made me
Cityless, made me wear these rags, which now
You weep to look on, now that you have come
Into the same grievous distress as I.
No need here for your tears: it is I must bear   1360
This burden while I live. You are my murderer,
You who have made me acquainted with this misery.
You thrust me out; you caused me thus to wander
Begging my daily sustenance from strangers.
Had these girls not been born to be my comfort,
I had been dead by now, for aught you cared.
But now these have preserved me, these my nurses,
These who are men, not women, in loving service.
But you two are some other's sons, not mine.
Therefore the Avenger's eyes are watching you,   1370
But not yet with so fierce a gaze as when
Those hosts move against Thebes. That city never
Can you overthrow. First you shall fall polluted
By the blood of your brother, and he with yours.

61

Such the curses I launched against you both,
And now invoke to fight upon my side,
That you may learn to revere parents, not
Utterly to scorn them, because a blind father
Begat such sons; for these maids did not thus.
So shall my curse defeat your 'suppliant rights',   1380
And your 'throne', if indeed primordial justice
Sits with Zeus, sanctioned by eternal laws.
Begone, loathed and unfathered by me, vilest
Of vile men, and take with you these my curses
Which I call down on you: never to vanquish
Your native land, nor ever to return
To hill-girt Argos, but by a kindred hand
To die, and slay him who has banished you.
Such my curse: and I call the dread primeval
Tartarean gloom to take you to its home;   1390
I call the Deities of this place, and Ares
Who has set this dire hate between you two.
Go, having heard this curse—go, publish it
To the Cadmeäns all, and to your own
Faithful allies; tell them how Oedipus
Has portioned out such honours to his sons.

LEADER
Polyneices, I liked not your former goings:
Now back to Argos get you gone with speed.

POLYNEICES
Alas for my journey and my hapless fortunes!
Alas for my comrades! What an end awaits   1400
Our sallying forth from Argos—woe is me!
Such an end that I may not utter it
To any of my friends, or turn them back,
But must in silence go to meet this doom.
Sisters, who are his daughters, you have heard
Your father's cruel prayers. Now by the Gods
I entreat you, if the curses of this father
Shall be fulfilled, and somehow you find means
To return home, do not dishonour me,
But give me burial and due funeral rites;   1410

So to the praise, which for your filial service
You now win, shall another praise as great
Be added, for this service done to me.

ANTIGONE
Polyneices, I entreat you, in one thing hear me.

POLYNEICES
What is that? Tell me, dearest Antigone.

ANTIGONE
Turn back your host to Argos with all speed,
And destroy not our city and yourself.

POLYNEICES
That were impossible. How could I again
Lead the same host when once I had shown fear?

ANTIGONE
But why, dear brother, should you grow wrath again?   1420
What will it profit you to lay waste your homeland?

POLYNEICES
Shameful is exile—and that I should thus
Be mocked by a brother, I the eldest-born.

ANTIGONE
See to what sure fulfilment you are bringing
His prophecies, who forebodes death for you both.

POLYNEICES
Yes, for he wishes it. But I must not yield.

ANTIGONE
Ay me!—And who will dare to follow you
When they have heard what prophecies he has uttered?

POLYNEICES
Why report evil tidings? A good leader
Should tell the better news and not the worse.   1430

ANTIGONE
Is it thus, brother, your resolve is fixed?

POLYNEICES
Yes—and detain me not. I now must tread
This omen-haunted path, driven to my doom

By my sire and his Furies. *Your* path, sisters,
May Zeus bless, if you fulfil, when I am dead,
My wishes; since you cannot while I live.
Release me now.—Farewell! for nevermore
Shall you behold me living.

ANTIGONE

               O sorrow, sorrow!

POLYNEICES
Mourn not for me.

ANTIGONE

           And who would not bewail you,
Brother, thus hastening to a death foreseen?   1440

POLYNEICES
If it must be, I shall die.

ANTIGONE

            Nay, hear my pleading...

POLYNEICES
Plead not against Fate.

ANTIGONE

            Woeful indeed am I,
If I must lose you.

POLYNEICES

           These things rest with Fortune—
Whether this way or that. But for you two,
May the Gods grant you never meet with evil;
For all men know that you deserve not suffering.

Exit POLYNEICES.

CHORUS
New evils are these that heavy with doom   *Strophe 1*
Come from the sightless stranger; unless perchance
It be but Fate finding its fulfilment.   1450
'Tis not for me to say that any of Heaven's ordinances
    are vain.
For watchful, ever watchful is Time:
Some will be overthrown; and again

64

On the morrow some will he lift high to honour.
   Thunder is heard.
Hark! The sky is thundering—O Zeus!

OEDIPUS
O children, children, is there not someone here
Whom we may send to summon Theseus hither?

ANTIGONE
And for what purpose, father, would you summon him?

OEDIPUS
This wingèd thunder of Zeus has come to lead me   1460
Forthwith to Hades. But send, send with speed.
   Thunder is heard again.

CHORUS
Again, louder it crashes down,   *Antistrophe 1*
The terrible bolt of thunder. The hair on my head
Stands on end for fear; my very soul
Is shaken with dismay, for again the lightning flashes
      from the sky.
With what event is it pregnant?
I am afraid; for never in vain
Does it burst forth, nor without disaster.   1470
   Thunder again.
O might of the great sky! O Zeus!

OEDIPUS
O children, upon your father now has come
His foretold end: no more can he escape it.

ANTIGONE
How know you? and what sign has told you this?

OEDIPUS
I know it well. But now let someone go
With all speed to the King, and fetch him hither.
   Thunder.

CHORUS
Again! hark, again!   *Strophe 2*
From all sides is heard

The terrible shattering din.
Be merciful, O strong God,
Be merciful, if on our dear
Motherland thou art bringing   1480
A dark withering storm.
Be gracious; nor, because I have looked on a man
    accurst, may I too share
With him some unblest,
Unearned recompense.
To thee do I cry, O Lord Zeus!

OEDIPUS
Is Theseus near? Still alive will he find me,
My children, and still master of my mind?

ANTIGONE
What is the pledge you would exchange with him?

OEDIPUS
In return for his benefits, gratefully
Would I pay that requital which I owe him.   1490

CHORUS
Oh come, my son, come hither   *Antistrophe 2*
In haste—if perchance
There in the innermost grove
With due sacrifice
Thou art hallowing the altar
Of the sea-god Poseidon—
Oh come thence, we pray thee.
For worthy of just recompense for benefits the stranger
    deems
Thyself to be, and yonder
City and all its folk.
Tarry not, O King. Come quickly.

Enter THESEUS.

THESEUS
What summons from you all once more do I hear—   1500
As clearly from my people as from my guest?
Can it be God's lightning, or a storm of hail

66

Bursting upon you? What might not our fears
Forebode, when Heaven sends such a storm as this?

OEDIPUS
Welcome is your coming, King. It is some God
Who has brought you hither by such happy fortune.

THESEUS
What new thing has befallen, son of Laïus?

OEDIPUS
My life hangs in the scale. I would die guiltless
Of a broken pledge to you and to your city.

THESEUS
For what sign of your fate may you be waiting?   1510

OEDIPUS
The Gods themselves are heralds of my doom,
Fulfilling every fore-appointed sign.

THESEUS
And what proofs do you find of this, old man?

OEDIPUS
The unceasing thunder, and the lightning hurled
Flash upon flash from the all-subduing hand.

THESEUS
It must be so. In you I find a prophet
Who speaks no falsehood. Say, what must be done.

OEDIPUS
Son of Aegeus, I will instruct you what to your city
Shall be a treasure which time cannot mar.
Forthwith, led by no guide's hand, I will show   1520
The way to that place wherein I must die.
Never to mortal man do thou reveal
The secret of that place, nor where it lies,
That so it may protect thee for all time
Better than many shields and succouring spears.
Its mysteries, by no speech profaned, thyself
Shalt learn, when to that place alone thou comest.
Neither to any of these citizens

67

May I declare them, nor to my own dear children.
Guard them always, till to the end of life   1530
Thou art come; then to thy heir alone shalt thou
Disclose them, and he shall teach them to his heir.
So thus unravaged by the Dragon's brood
Shall be your land. For slight cause will most cities
Assault a neighbour, be she ne'er so just.
For the Gods are slow, but sure, to visit sin,
When scorning righteousness men turn to folly.
Swerve you not so from wisdom, son of Aegeus.
But such things you know well without my warnings.
Now to that place—for the God's call urges me—   1540
Let us set forth, and hesitate no more.
Follow me, children; for in strange wise now
Have I become your guide, as you were mine.
Come then, forward! Touch me not, but leave me
Unaided to find out that sacred tomb
Where fate will give me burial in this land.
This way—come—this way! for so guiding Hermes
Is leading me, and the Goddess of the dead.
O Light—no Light to me—mine wast thou once,
But now for the last time my body feels thee.   1550
For now I go to hide my life's ending
With Hades.—But, O dearest of all friends,
May thou and this thy land and all its people
Be blest; and in prosperity remember
Me, the dead, and be fortunate evermore.

Exit OEDIPUS, *followed by his* DAUGHTERS *and*
THESEUS *and* ATTENDANTS.

CHORUS
If without sacrilege   *Strophe*
I may adore with prayer
The unknown Goddess, and thee,
Thou Lord of the people of night,
Aidoneus, Aidoneus, hear, oh hear!   1560
Painlessly, not by a death that awakes
Lamentation, may the wanderer pass
Down to the all-enshrouding fields

Of the dead below, to the Stygian house.
Much sorrow came to him undeserved;
But in requital a just God
Will lift him up once again to honour.

Goddesses of Underworld,   *Antistrophe*
Thou too, unconquered monster,
Terrible shape, who lairest
In the gates where all must pass,   1570
Thou Guardian untameable of Hades,
Snarling at all from the jaws of thy cavern,
As ancient story tells!
O Death, son of Earth and of Tartarus,
I entreat that the wanderer now may move
In a clear path upon his way
Down to the nether fields of the dead.
To thee I call, giver of sleep eternal.

Enter MESSENGER.

MESSENGER
My countrymen, briefly will I sum up
The news I bring you: Oedipus is gone.   1580
But in no brief words may the tale be told
Of all those many strange things that befell.

LEADER
He is dead then, that poor unhappy man?

MESSENGER
Yes; his long life of misery is over.

LEADER
But how? by a god-sent and a painless death?

MESSENGER
Ah there we come to what must move our wonder.
You who were present saw how from this place
He set forth, with no friend guiding his steps,
But he himself showing the way to us all.
Now when to the steep Threshold he had come,   1590
By a brazen stairway rooted deep in the earth,

69

In one of many branching paths he halted,
Near the rock-basin, where the inviolate
Pledges of Theseus and Peirithoüs lie.
Midway he stood between the hollow pear-tree,
The tomb of stone, and the Thorician rock;
Then sat down, and stripped off his sordid garments.
And then he called to his daughters, bade them fetch
Spring-water that he might wash and pour libation.
To plant-fostering Demeter's neighbouring hill   1600
They went, and in short space of time brought back
The water as their father bade, wherewith
They washed and dressed him as the rite prescribes.
But when he was content, all being done,
And naught of his desire neglected, then
Chthonian Zeus thundered; and when they heard,
The maidens shuddered: at their father's knees
Weeping they bowed their heads, unceasingly
Beating their breasts and keening with loud wails.
And when he heard their sudden bitter cries,   1610
He clasped his arms around them and said, 'O children,
From this day you will no more have a father.
All that was mine has perished; and no more
Need you endure the burden of tending me—
A heavy burden, I know it well, my daughters;
Yet one word cancels all this toil: such love
As you have had from me, from no man else
Have you received: and now bereft of me
Shall you live on through all your days to come.'
Thus folded each within the others' arms   1620
They wept and sobbed. But when they had made an end
Of lamentation, and their cries had ceased,
There was a silence; then a voice suddenly
Was heard as of one calling, and straightway
The hair of our heads stood up, with terror thrilled.
For many times the God called him in many ways:
'O thou—thou—Oedipus! wherefore delay we
To go? Too long hast thou been tarrying here.'
And when he knew the God was summoning him,
He asked that our king Theseus should come near him,   1630

And when he came, spoke thus: 'O my friend, give
Thy right hand to my children in solemn pledge,
And you, daughters, to him; and promise never
Willingly to forsake them, but in kindness
At all times to protect and succour them.'
And he, too noble to give way to tears,
Sware he would keep that promise to his friend.
When Theseus had done this, at once Oedipus
Touched his children with blind hands, and said:
'Children, you must endure with noble courage,   1640
And depart from this place, nor claim to behold
Unlawful sights, or hear what shall be said.
Then depart straightway. Only let King Theseus
Remain to witness what shall now be done.'
These words he spoke; and hearing them, we all
Followed the maidens with fast-falling tears
And lamentations: but soon, as we went,
We looked back, and saw Oedipus indeed
No longer present anywhere, but alone
The King, holding his hand before his face   1650
To screen his eyes, as if some awful thing
Had happened, unendurable to behold.
Then after a brief time we saw him first
Bend down and do obeisance to the earth,
Then to the sky where dwell the Gods above.
But by what manner of death Oedipus perished,
No mortal man can tell, save Theseus only.
For neither in that hour did any bolt
Of fire, sent by the God, destroy his life,
Nor any whirlwind rising from the sea;   1660
But either the Gods took him; or earth's caves
Were riven, and gave him a kind painless death:
For not saddened by sickness was his passing,
Nor by laments, but, beyond mortal wont,
Most wonderful. And if my tale seem folly,
I dispute not with those who count me foolish.

LEADER
Where are the maidens and their friendly escort?

71

MESSENGER
Yonder not far; for sounds of lamentation
Clearly announce that they will soon be with us.

Enter ANTIGONE *and* ISMENE.

ANTIGONE
Ah woe, woe! Now indeed our fate it is,   *Strophe 1* 1670
Now more than ever before to bewail
The accursed blood born in us from our father.
Many the miseries
Which in the past without pause we have borne for him;
Now at the last such a vision of terror,
Such a loss is ours to tell of.

CHORUS
What mean you?

ANTIGONE
                    Nay, we can but conjecture, friends.
CHORUS
He is gone . . .

ANTIGONE
                    By such a death as you might wish for him.
Neither in war, nor on the deep
Did a sudden fate arrest him;   1680
But by a swift invisible doom
Away was he snatched down to the dim fields of the dead.
And now, alas, upon our eyes
Falls a darkness as of death. For how should ever she
        and I
Find a wretched livelihood, as through some far-off land
        we roam,
Or over the billows of the sea?

ISMENE
Nay I know not. Would but the pitiless
House of Hades join me in death
Unto my aged father!   1690
Ah woe is me! I cannot live
The life that is now my portion.

CHORUS
Sisterly pair, O best of daughters, Heaven's decree must
    be endured.
Be not aflame with too much grief.
No cause is here for repining.

ANTIGONE
Regret, then, for past distress there may be.   *Antistrophe 1*
That which in no way was happy had happiness,
While still with my embrace I might console him.
Father so dear to me,   1700
Though now in Hell's nether murk ever shrouded,
Yet not even there shall you cease to be comforted
By the love of your two children.

CHORUS
He hath fared...

ANTIGONE
            Aye, fared even as he himself would wish.

CHORUS
But how?

ANTIGONE
            Within a foreign land, the land he chose,
Here hath he died. A secret grave
Hideth his repose for ever.
Weeping friends he has left to mourn him:
For from my eyes, father, the tears fall to the ground
As I bewail thee; nor do I know   1710
How I may subdue my grief, this grief for thee that is
    so great.
Woe is me! Thy wish it was to die in a strange land;
    but now
By me unhonoured is thy tomb.

ISMENE
O my sorrow! What are the miseries,
What new fate forlorn and lone,
Awaiting thee and me, dear sister,
Fatherless friendless orphans?

73

CHORUS

Nay, dear children, since your sire has won to a blessed
    end of life,   1720
Cease your lament; for of mortal men
Few may escape ill-fortune.

ANTIGONE
Dear sister, let us hasten back...   *Strophe 2*

ISMENE

But to what end?

ANTIGONE
A longing assails me...

ISMENE

For what?

ANTIGONE
Once more to behold that dark abode...

ISMENE
But whose?

ANTIGONE

Our father's—oh despair!

ISMENE
But how can that be lawful? Sister,
Do you not see?

ANTIGONE

Oh why reprove me?   1730

ISMENE
This besides...

ANTIGONE

What more would you tell me?

ISMENE
Tombless he vanished, with none to be witness.

ANTIGONE
Lead me thither, then slay me also.

ISMENE
Ai ai!
Wretched maiden, where now,
Where thus helpless, lonely and desolate,
Shall I live out my sad life?

CHORUS
Fear naught, dear children.   *Antistrophe 2*

ISMENE
                    Ah but whither am I to flee?

CHORUS
Already a refuge you found
That from disaster saved your lives.   1740

ISMENE
I know it.

CHORUS
          What then is thy thought?

ISMENE
How we may find our way to Thebes
I cannot tell.

CHORUS
          But why should you seek it?

ISMENE
Trouble besets us.

CHORUS
                Not for the first time.

ISMENE
Desperate then; but today we are hopeless.

CHORUS
Verily great is the sea of your troubles.

ISMENE
Zeus, Zeus!
Whither shall we turn now?
Vain are hopes: not one remains to me.
Where, where will Fate now drive us?   1750

Enter THESEUS.

THESEUS
Children, weep no more. Such a grace,
Bestowed by the quick and the dead by the Dark Powers,
Let none mourn, lest they provoke wrath.

ANTIGONE

O son of Aegeus, humbly we beg thee...

THESEUS

What boon would you have me grant you, my children?

ANTIGONE

With our own eyes fain would we gaze on the tomb
Where our father is laid.

THESEUS

                  That were unlawful.

ANTIGONE

What say you, O King, despot of Athens?

THESEUS

My children, he gave me charge to allow   1760
No mortal man to approach that place
Nor address with prayer that sacred tomb
Wherein your father sleeping is laid.
And while, so he said, I obeyed his behest,
By foes unharmed still should my land be.
Thus did I swear, and was heard by the God,
And the all-knowing Guardian of oath-plight.

ANTIGONE

Nay if this be pleasing to him, why then
This should content us. But now to the ancient
City of Thebes send us, if haply   1770
By our pleading we so may avert this bloodshed
Threatening our brothers.

THESEUS

This will I do; and will spare no pains
If in aught I may help you, or pleasure the spirit
Of him who of late has departed.

CHORUS

Come, for laments there is no more need:
Then cease to bewail him;
For the will of the Gods is accomplished.

Printed in the United States
By Bookmasters